Curly
and the Honey

Tony Mitton

Illustrated by Andy Parker

Here comes Curly creeping along, singing a sweet little caterpillar song.

What does he see?

He sees a busy bee.

Here comes Curly peeping round a tree.
What does he see?

He sees a lot of bees
buzzing in the tree.

Here comes Curly wriggling
on the branch. What does he see
hiding in the tree?

He sees a hive of honey!

Here comes Curly.

He gives the hive a tap.

Plip! Plop! Plap!
Out falls a drop of
lovely runny honey.

Here come Curly's friends,
one, two, three.
"We are very hungry.
Is there anything for tea?"

"Look," says Curly.

"There's honey for tea!"

"Clever old Curly!
We like honey for tea!"